S0-BCV-405

AND *God Saw*
That It Was
GOOD

GENESIS 1:18

AND *God Saw* That It Was GOOD

GENESIS 1:18

INSPIRING LISTS JOURNAL

DAYMAKER™
An Imprint of Barbour Publishing, Inc.

© 2015 by Barbour Publishing, Inc.

Written and compiled by Karin Dahl Silver.

ISBN 978-1-63058-720-8

All rights reserved. No part of this publication may be reproduced or transmitted for commercial purposes, except for brief quotations in printed reviews, without written permission of the publisher.

Churches and other noncommercial interests may reproduce portions of this book without the express written permission of Barbour Publishing, provided that the text does not exceed 500 words or 5 percent of the entire book, whichever is less, and that the text is not material quoted from another publisher. When reproducing text from this book, include the following credit line: "From *And God Saw That It Was Good: Inspiring Lists Journal*, published by Barbour Publishing, Inc. Used by permission."

Published by DayMaker, an imprint of Barbour Publishing, Inc., P.O. Box 719, Uhrichsville, Ohio 44683, www.barbourbooks.com

Our mission is to publish and distribute inspirational products offering exceptional value and biblical encouragement to the masses.

Member of the
Evangelical Christian
Publishers Association

Printed in the United States of America.

MY
"Life Verse"
LIST

_____
_____
_____
_____
_____
_____
_____
_____
_____
_____
_____
_____
_____
_____
_____
_____
_____
_____
_____
_____
_____
_____
_____
_____
_____

MY
"Where I've Seen God Working in My Life"
LIST

_____

_____

_____

_____

_____

_____

_____

_____

_____

_____

_____

_____

_____

_____

_____

_____

_____

MY
"Times I Have Felt God's Nearness"
LIST

MY
"Puzzling Questions I Have for God"
LIST

MY
"I Always Thank God For. . ."
LIST

· ·

_____

_____

_____

_____

_____

_____

_____

_____

_____

_____

_____

_____

_____

_____

_____

_____

_____

_____

_____

_____

_____

_____

_____

_____

MY
"I Pray Hardest When. . ."
LIST

· ·

_____

_____

_____

_____

_____

_____

_____

_____

_____

_____

_____

_____

_____

_____

_____

_____

_____

_____

_____

_____

_____

_____

MY
"God Must Have a Sense of Humor Because..."
LIST

MY
"I Know God Loves Me Because. . ."
LIST

MY
"Family Members Who Inspire Me"
LIST

MY
"Smells and Sounds That Bring Back Old Memories"
LIST

_____
_____
_____
_____
_____
_____
_____
_____
_____
_____
_____
_____
_____
_____
_____
_____
_____
_____
_____

MY
"Heroes, Real or Fictional"
LIST

MY
"I Wish I Could Be More _____"
LIST

MY
"Best Lessons I've Learned from Difficult Situations"
LIST

MY
"Books That Inspire Me"
LIST

· ·

_____

_____

_____

_____

_____

_____

_____

_____

_____

_____

_____

_____

_____

_____

_____

_____

_____

_____

_____

_____

_____

_____

MY
"Books I Keep Meaning to Read"
LIST

_____
_____
_____
_____
_____
_____
_____
_____
_____
_____
_____
_____
_____
_____
_____
_____
_____

MY
"Quotes That Inspire Me"
LIST

· ·

_____

_____

_____

_____

_____

_____

_____

_____

_____

_____

_____

_____

_____

_____

_____

_____

_____

_____

_____

_____

_____

_____

_____

_____

MY
"Languages I Wish I Could Speak"
LIST

MY
"Favorite Movies"
LIST

MY
"Fictional Worlds I'd Like to Visit"
LIST

MY
"Creative Gifts"
LIST

MY
"Famous Artwork I'd Love to See in Person"
LIST

MY
"Places I'd Love to Visit"
LIST

_____
_____
_____
_____
_____
_____
_____
_____
_____
_____
_____
_____
_____
_____
_____
_____
_____
_____
_____
_____
_____
_____
_____
_____
_____
_____
_____
_____

MY
"The Most Beautiful Parts of Creation"
LIST

MY
"Favorite Types of Weather"
LIST

MY
"Most Dangerous Weather Experiences"
LIST

· ·

_____

_____

_____

_____

_____

_____

_____

_____

_____

_____

_____

_____

_____

_____

_____

_____

_____

_____

_____

_____

_____

_____

_____

_____

_____

_____

_____

_____

_____

MY
"Grossest Experiences with Nature"
LIST

· ·

_____

_____

_____

_____

_____

_____

_____

_____

_____

_____

_____

_____

_____

_____

_____

_____

_____

_____

_____

_____

_____

MY
"Awe-Inspiring Experiences with Nature"
LIST

· ·

_____

_____

_____

_____

_____

_____

_____

_____

_____

_____

_____

_____

_____

_____

_____

_____

_____

_____

_____

_____

_____

_____

_____

MY
"How I Care for God's Creation"
LIST

MY
"How I Share God's Love"
LIST

MY
"Awkward Situations That Are Now Funny in Retrospect"
LIST

. . . .

MY
"Things About Me That Surprise Other People"
LIST

· ·

_____

_____

_____

_____

_____

_____

_____

_____

_____

_____

_____

_____

_____

_____

_____

_____

_____

_____

_____

_____

_____

MY
"Character Qualities I Want to Cultivate"
LIST

· ·

_____

_____

_____

_____

_____

_____

_____

_____

_____

_____

_____

_____

_____

_____

_____

_____

_____

_____

_____

_____

_____

_____

_____

_____

_____

_____

MY
"Compliments That Made Me Beam"
LIST

MY
"Best Thinking Spots"
LIST

_____
_____
_____
_____
_____
_____
_____
_____
_____
_____
_____
_____
_____
_____
_____
_____
_____
_____
_____

MY
"I'm Curious About. . ."
LIST

· ·

MY
"Things That Amaze Me About the Human Body"
LIST

· ·

_____

_____

_____

_____

_____

_____

_____

_____

_____

_____

_____

_____

_____

_____

_____

_____

_____

_____

_____

_____

_____

_____

MY
"I Never Thought I Could, but I Totally Did It!"
LIST

MY
"What Inspires Me to Leave My Comfort Zone"
LIST

· ·

_____

_____

_____

_____

_____

_____

_____

_____

_____

_____

_____

_____

_____

_____

_____

_____

_____

_____

_____

_____

_____

_____

_____

_____

_____

_____

MY
"Friends Who Encourage Me to Keep Going and Growing"
LIST

MY
"Teachers Who Have Made an Impact on Me"
LIST

· ·

MY
"What Inspires Me to Serve Others"
LIST

MY
"Goals and Dreams"
LIST

· ·

_____

_____

_____

_____

_____

_____

_____

_____

_____

_____

_____

_____

_____

_____

_____

_____

_____

_____

MY
"Accomplishments I'm Proud Of"
LIST

MY
"Amazing Answers to Prayer"
LIST

MY
"Stories in the Bible I Struggle With"
LIST

MY
"Stories in the Bible That Strengthen My Faith"
LIST

- -

MY
"I Can See God's Handiwork In. . ."
LIST

MY
"Favorite Things About the Seasons Changing"
LIST

MY
"If I Could Be Any Animal for One Day, I Would Be. . ."
LIST

MY
"Mysteries of Nature I Wonder About"
LIST

· ·

_____

_____

_____

_____

_____

_____

_____

_____

_____

_____

_____

_____

_____

_____

_____

_____

_____

_____

_____

_____

MY
"What I Wanted to Be When I Grew Up"
LIST

MY
"Dream Careers"
LIST

- -

MY
"People Whose Work Ethic Inspires Me"
LIST

MY
"Organizations That Give Me Faith in Humanity"
LIST

· ·

_____

_____

_____

_____

_____

_____

_____

_____

_____

_____

_____

_____

_____

_____

_____

_____

_____

_____

_____

_____

_____

_____

_____

_____

_____

_____

_____

MY
"Inspiring Leaders, Past and Present"
LIST

· ·

_____

_____

_____

_____

_____

_____

_____

_____

_____

_____

_____

_____

_____

_____

_____

_____

_____

MY
"What I Love About My Country"
LIST

MY
"Favorite Time Periods in History"
LIST

MY
"Modern Marvels I'm Thankful For"
LIST

• •

_____

_____

_____

_____

_____

_____

_____

_____

_____

_____

_____

_____

_____

_____

_____

_____

MY
"I Couldn't Live Without..."
LIST

MY
"Physical Activities That Fire Me Up"
LIST

· ·

MY
"Fitness Goals"
LIST

MY
"How to Get Myself Up and Moving"
LIST

MY
"Most Inspiring Olympic Sports to Watch"
LIST

. . . .

MY
"Sports I'd Like to Learn How to Play"
LIST

MY
"Amazing Feats I've Seen Others Accomplish"
LIST

MY
"Sights That Have Taken My Breath Away"
LIST

· ·

MY
"Music That Stirs My Soul"
LIST

MY
"Best Songs for Cheering Up a Bad Day"
LIST

MY
"Comfort Foods"
LIST

MY
"Things I Wish Were Different About the World"
LIST

. . . .

_____

_____

_____

_____

_____

_____

_____

_____

_____

_____

_____

_____

_____

_____

_____

_____

_____

_____

_____

_____

_____

_____

MY
"Saddest Movies I've Ever Seen"
LIST

MY
"Movies That Defined My Childhood"
LIST

MY
"Internet Videos That Always Make Me Laugh"
LIST

MY
"Corny Jokes That Are Actually Hilarious"
LIST

MY
"If I Were Fearless, I Would. . ."
LIST

MY

"If Money Were No Object, I Would. . ."

LIST

· ·

MY
"Things That Ignite My Righteous Anger"
LIST

MY
"Pet Peeves"
LIST

MY
"Times I Have Doubted Myself"
LIST

· ·

_____

_____

_____

_____

_____

_____

_____

_____

_____

_____

_____

_____

_____

_____

_____

_____

_____

_____

MY
"Times When Encouragement Arrived Right on Time"
LIST

• •

_____

_____

_____

_____

_____

_____

_____

_____

_____

_____

_____

_____

_____

_____

_____

_____

_____

_____

_____

_____

_____

_____

_____

_____

_____

MY
"Worst Advice I've Ever Been Given"
LIST

MY
"Best Advice I've Ever Heard"
LIST

MY
"Love Is. . ."
LIST

· ·

_____
_____
_____
_____
_____
_____
_____
_____
_____
_____
_____
_____
_____
_____
_____
_____
_____
_____
_____
_____
_____
_____
_____
_____
_____
_____
_____
_____

MY
"I Feel Most Loved When. . ."
LIST

MY
"My Friends' Character Traits That Inspire Me"
LIST

MY
"How My Closest Friends Earned My Trust"
LIST

MY
"God's Character Traits That Inspire Me"
LIST

- -

_____

_____

_____

_____

_____

_____

_____

_____

_____

_____

_____

_____

_____

_____

_____

_____

_____

_____

_____

_____

MY
"Ways I Want to Grow in My Relationships"
LIST

MY
"Books of the Bible I've Read Over and Over"
LIST

· ·

MY
"Books That Helped Me Understand Myself Better"
LIST

· ·

_____

_____

_____

_____

_____

_____

_____

_____

_____

_____

_____

_____

_____

_____

_____

_____

_____

_____

MY
"Most Inspiring Authors and Artists"
LIST

· ·

_____

_____

_____

_____

_____

_____

_____

_____

_____

_____

_____

_____

_____

_____

_____

_____

_____

_____

_____

_____

_____

_____

MY
"I Would Love to Learn How to Make..."
LIST

MY
"Talents I Admire"
LIST

MY
"Gifts and Talents I See in Myself"
LIST

· ·

MY
"Hobbies and Activites That Enrich My Life"
LIST

MY
"Best Games for Groups"
LIST

· ·

MY
"Activities Where I Get Super Competitive"
LIST

MY
"What I Doodle When I'm Bored"
LIST

MY
"When I'm Feeling Anxious, I. . ."
LIST

· ·

_____
_____
_____
_____
_____
_____
_____
_____
_____
_____
_____
_____
_____
_____
_____
_____
_____
_____
_____
_____
_____
_____
_____
_____
_____
_____

MY
"What I'm Most Afraid Of"
LIST

MY
"Creatures That Creep Me Out"
LIST

· ·

MY
"Lies I Tell Myself When I'm Hurting"
LIST

· ·

_____

_____

_____

_____

_____

_____

_____

_____

_____

_____

_____

_____

_____

_____

_____

_____

_____

_____

_____

_____

_____

_____

MY
"Truths I Need to Hear Every Day"
LIST

MY
"Failures That Inspired Me to Try Harder"
LIST

MY
"Encouraging Promises from Scripture"
LIST

MY
"Most Embarrassing Moments"
LIST

· ·

MY
"Most Daring Moments"
LIST

MY
"Secrets I've Told (and Why I Told Them)"
LIST

MY
"Hardest Times to Tell the Truth"
LIST

MY
"I Am Very Protective Of. . ."
LIST

MY
"How to Love Others Well"
LIST

MY
"Recipe for a Relaxing Day"
LIST

MY
"Best Pep-Talks I've Given Myself"
LIST

· ·

MY
"Beauty Is. . ."
LIST

MY
"Everyday Glimpses of Beauty"
LIST

MY
"Things I Love About My Body"
LIST

· ·

_____

_____

_____

_____

_____

_____

_____

_____

_____

_____

_____

_____

_____

_____

_____

_____

_____

_____

_____

_____

_____

_____

_____

MY
"Things I'd Like to Change About My Body"
LIST

MY
"I Want to Dance When I Hear. . ."
LIST

· ·

_____

_____

_____

_____

_____

_____

_____

_____

_____

_____

_____

_____

_____

_____

_____

_____

_____

_____

_____

_____

_____

_____

_____

MY
"Songs I Can't Help Singing Along With"
LIST

MY
"Musicians Who Inspire Me"
LIST

· ·

MY
"Favorite Worship Songs and Hymns"
LIST

· ·

_____

_____

_____

_____

_____

_____

_____

_____

_____

_____

_____

_____

_____

_____

_____

_____

_____

_____

_____

_____

_____

_____

MY
"Most Soothing Sounds in Nature"
LIST

· ·

MY
"For a Good Night's Sleep, I Need. . ."
LIST

MY
"For a Good Morning, I Need. . ."
LIST

MY
"Favorite Places and Times to Talk with God"
LIST

MY
"Doubts I've Had About My Faith"
LIST

· ·

MY
"Ways God Has Helped Me with My Doubts"
LIST

. . . .

_____

_____

_____

_____

_____

_____

_____

_____

_____

_____

_____

_____

_____

_____

_____

_____

_____

_____

_____

MY
"I Put All of My Heart Into. . ."
LIST

· ·

_____

_____

_____

_____

_____

_____

_____

_____

_____

_____

_____

_____

_____

_____

_____

_____

_____

_____

_____

_____

MY
"Social Issues That Are Important to Me"
LIST

MY
"Movies and Art That Changed the Way I Look at the World"
LIST

MY
"World-Changing Events That Shocked Me When They Happened"
LIST

MY
"I Feel Compassion For..."
LIST

MY
"I'm Inspired to Give Generously When..."
LIST

MY
"I'm Saving Up For. . ."
LIST

MY
"I Won't Give Up On. . ."
LIST

MY
"Courage Is. . ."
LIST

· ·

_____

_____

_____

_____

_____

_____

_____

_____

_____

_____

_____

_____

_____

_____

_____

_____

_____

_____

_____

_____

MY
"Bravest Things I've Ever Done"
LIST

MY
"Friendships That Have Survived Hard Times"
LIST

MY
"What Makes a Place Feel Like Home"
LIST

MY
"Work That Inspires Me"
LIST

MY
"Ways I Want to Grow in My Talents or Work"
LIST

MY
"Activities That Help Me Refocus When I'm Stressed Out"
LIST

MY
"Wonders of the Natural World"
LIST

· ·

_____

_____

_____

_____

_____

_____

_____

_____

_____

_____

_____

_____

_____

_____

_____

_____

_____

_____

_____

_____

_____

_____

_____

MY
"Wonders of the Man-Made World"
LIST

MY
"Times I've Felt Closest to God"
LIST

MY
"Spiritual Leaders Who Have Inspired Me"
LIST

MY
"Trials That Strengthened My Faith"
LIST

MY
"Favorite Views of the Sky"
LIST

· ·

_____

_____

_____

_____

_____

_____

_____

_____

_____

_____

_____

_____

_____

_____

_____

_____

_____

_____

_____

_____

_____

_____

_____

MY
"Places That Make Me Feel Small"
LIST

· ·

MY
"Times When I've Felt Most Alive"
LIST

MY
"Recurring Daydreams"
LIST

MY
"Worries That Keep Me Awake at Night"
LIST

MY
"Really Weird Dreams I've Had"
LIST

· ·

MY
"Favorite Plants to Stop and Smell"
LIST

· ·

_____

_____

_____

_____

_____

_____

_____

_____

_____

_____

_____

_____

_____

_____

_____

_____

_____

_____

MY
"Creatures That Are Fascinating to Watch"
LIST

MY
"God. . .Why Did You Create That?"
LIST

MY
"I Can't Help Laughing When..."
LIST

MY
"Impressive Meals I Know How to Make"
LIST

MY
"Strangest Foods I've Tried"
LIST

· ·

MY
"I Can't Put Off Grocery Shopping Anymore If I'm Out Of. . ."
LIST

MY
"I Absolutely Have to Clean When _____ Is Dirty"
LIST

MY
"I Want to Learn More About. . ."
LIST

MY
"Intelligent People Who Inspire Me"
LIST

MY
"I Hope _____ Gets Invented Soon"
LIST

· ·

_____

_____

_____

_____

_____

_____

_____

_____

_____

_____

_____

_____

_____

_____

_____

_____

_____

_____

_____

_____

_____

_____

_____

_____

_____

MY
"Things I Miss from When I Was Little"
LIST

MY
"What Will Heaven Be Like?"
LIST

· ·

_____

_____

_____

_____

_____

_____

_____

_____

_____

_____

_____

_____

_____

_____

_____

_____

_____

_____

_____

_____

_____

_____

_____

_____

_____

MY
"Bible Verses I Want to Memorize"
LIST

MY
"I Feel the Joy of the Lord When. . ."
LIST

- -

MY
"Fruits of the Spirit I'm Working On"
LIST

MY
"I Knew I Was Growing Up When. . ."
LIST

· ·

_____

_____

_____

_____

_____

_____

_____

_____

_____

_____

_____

_____

_____

_____

_____

_____

_____

MY
"Tips for Living a Whole-Hearted Life"
LIST

MY
"In the Future, I Hope I'm. . ."
LIST

· ·

_____

_____

_____

_____

_____

_____

_____

_____

_____

_____

_____

_____

_____

_____

_____

_____

_____

_____

_____

_____

_____

_____

_____

_____

_____

_____

_____

_____